FREDA Ai

I KNOW WHAT WHAT YOU ARE GOING THROUGH

HE FIVE LETTER WORD CALLED GRIEF

outskirts
press

I would like to dedicate this book to my Lord and Savior Jesus Christ. Without him I am absolutely nothing.

Philippians 4:13

I can do all things through Christ which strengthens me.

TABLE OF CONTENTS

INTRODUCTION

Matthew 25:13

"Watch therefore, for you know neither the day nor
the hour in which the Son of Man is coming."

I can remember New Years Day, January 1, 2009. We were at my cousin's house celebrating the New Year. When the New Year came in, we hugged and celebrated. The one moment that stuck out was when my husband, Curtis, told me over and over again, "09 IS MINE, BABY." He wanted to continue to focus on his businesses and make it work, and he always wanted me to be a stay-at-home mom. I truly appreciated him trying. He was a sweetheart. However, what life has taught me is to enjoy every single moment of your life and how not to take any moment for granted. I use to say, "Just take day by day." Now I say, "Take moment by moment."

I used to wonder how people could go on about their regular lives while I was hurting and going through a never-ending moment of my life. My husband gone. My world stopped. My dreams stopped. I didn't know how I was going to go on. How was I going to make it? Who was going to help me raise our kids? (Because he was so good at it.) We traveled together, we had goals together, we worshipped God together, we wanted to see our grandkids together, EVERYTHING JUST STOPPED in a blink of an eye. Can I say that "I TRULY KNOW WHAT YOU ARE GOING THROUGH!"

SIGNIFICANT THINGS ABOUT THE DAY CURTIS WENT TO HEAVEN

It was January 18, 2009 around 5:00 in the morning. Curtis and I began enjoying some pillow talk. He said to me, "Baby, how long have we been together?" I said, "Well, your baby sister was nineteen and we been together since she was eleven months old and we've been married since 1995. So I did the calculations and said, "We been together for eighteen years and married for fourteen and a half years."

Curtis replied very overjoyed, "And I enjoyed every last moment with you." And not thinking that this could be my last few hours with him, I responded, "Well, we're going to have many, many more."

When I got up that morning at 10:00 a.m. I made some oatmeal. We both ate our bowl of oatmeal in bed. We loved oatmeal, especially on those cold winter mornings. After he ate the oatmeal, he said, "You know, you make the best oatmeal."

I said, "Awwwww, Baby, you just trying to pump me up—but I am so happy you enjoyed it." I didn't get too skeptical because he was always complimenting me and making me feel good, even within the smallest things. That's why I loved him.

Just before I was about to go to Sam's Club around 12:00 noon to get food for our football party (Baltimore Ravens vs. Pittsburgh) and President Obama party, which was on January 20, 2009, Curtis told me that if anything ever happened to him, to live out his legacy and take care of our kids. Now enough was enough. I said "Stop talking like that; you are going to be here to take care of our kids, see our grand-kids, graduations, college and everything else."

He then hugged me very tight and told me he loved me. Then he gave me a list of food items to get for our celebrations. Of course, I never asked myself, "Could this be the last conversation we will have?" I would have taken him to the store with me or stayed home. I know I would not have left him. We always confessed our love for each other and for our children all the time. So, I just figured that he was having a sentimental moment. We both did that periodically. But I didn't take it that it was our very last moment. The very last time I would see him talk, smile, laugh, hug…and the list goes on and on. I really took it for granted.

Another thing I thought about later is the fact that most of the time I don't usually take all the kids with me when I go to the market but I did this day. They all wanted to go. Life is something else when you look back on everything that has happened. Trust me, I know what you are going through.

I went to the market and as I was driving, we were talking on the phone, in the store we were talking on the phone, and right until we were on our way back home at 2:30 p.m. I continued calling Curtis to see what he was doing but he didn't answer the phone. My mind began racing because he always answers my calls. I have always been a worry wart. I sped home with the kids, and groceries in the car. My stomach began to hurt. I began thinking about the conversation we had this morning, "take care of my kid and live out my legacy". Once I pulled in front of the house, My brother-in-law was sitting in his parked car in front of the house when we arrived. I ran into the house looking for my husband. Upstairs, no Curtis. I went to the basement. As I went down the steps, I observed Curtis lying on the sofa asleep. His phone was propped by his ear. I let out a sigh of relief, thanking God that he was sleeping. I said, "Curty." No response. I ran over to him and said, "Curty." That is when his arm fell to his side. I looked at his face very carefully and his face and tongue was dry looking. I immediately panicked. I cried out. My brother in law called 911. As he called 911 I checked Curtis' pulse; there was no pulse, no breathing. Some way God enabled me to pick up my 250 lb. husband and place him on the floor and I immediately started CPR. It seemed like forever; every time I would breathe into him I thought he was alive--that his heart would jump start back to beating. I thought he was coming back, so I never stopped. I heard gurgling. I was getting so happy. I was like *if the ambulance hurries up and get here, they can shock him and get him going.* I was praying so hard. I was like *Come on, Jesus, please help him. Come on, please.* The ambulance came and took him to Union Memorial hospital. It was so cold outside. I can remember all my kids eyes were wide with fear as we'd tried to bring our loved one back to life. My kids at the time were 15, 11, 4, and 1. I remember some of my neighbors in the front of my house praying.

It was a very sad day, very cold. Lifeless. Hopeless. Helpless day. Curtis passed away from a sudden heart attack. What the heck? Unbelievable. Totally unexpected. Let me tell you, "I KNOW WHAT YOU ARE GOING THROUGH." Whether you are prepared or unprepared for your loved one passing, losing your loved one will feel like your world is over.

The purpose of this book journal is to help guide you through this unimaginable process of grief. There is no time limit on grief. There are no rules. The loss and the emptiness that you are feeling right now is real and without a doubt it hurts like no other. I had no clue what people went through after a loss until I lost someone that was close and dear to me. This book is designed so that you can participate by writing your feelings down; this will be your very own story. This will also be a guide for you during this season. One day in the future you will look back in your journal you created and admire how far you came. I want this book to be your story. Trust and Faith in God will pull you through.

Matthew 5:4

"Blessed are those who mourn,
for they will be comforted."

Chapter 1

———∽∾∽———

THE DAY OUR LOVED ONE PASSED

AT THE HOSPITAL, I can remember there were a lot of family and friends present. I remember lots of sadness and tears. I can't remember who all was there. All I could think about was my babies having no daddy and me having no husband. His parents having no son. His siblings having no brother, his nieces and nephews having no uncle. Oh, and I can't forget his close friends and his mentor kids. Everyone would be affected. Then I'd go back to my children. How were we going to survive and make it? I was angry. I was in shock. I was in disbelief. I was just done with everything including my life.

What was so significant about January 18, 2009 was, first, that it was a Sunday. It was the Sunday of the Baltimore vs Pittsburgh football game so we were having a little football party that day.

January 20, 2009 was President Barack Obama's inauguration. We were having another party because we were so excited for President Obama. Curtis followed President Obama since he was a Senator and he said three years before he ran that he was going to be the President.

He loved politics and he was elated that President Obama was elected. I will never forget that moment.

The very next day after my husband passed away it snowed. My husband had been waiting for snow so he could take the kids sledding over Lake Montebello.

What was significant about the day you lost your loved one? Where were you? When was it? How were you feeling? What were you doing prior to losing your loved one?

_____

_____

_____

_____

_____

_____

_____

_____

_____

_____

_____

_____

_____

_____

_____

_____

_____

_____

_____

_____

_____

_____

_____

_____

_____

_____

_____

_____

_____

_____

Chapter 2

―――∽∾∾――――

PLANNING THE FUNERAL

PLANNING THE FUNERAL really gave me mixed emotions. Now that I think about it, I felt like I was all over the place. Running to the funeral home, cemetery, trying to plan the repast, getting the programs, flowers, his outfit and pictures together. I remember trying to make sure everyone was ok and comfortable. I remember in between all of that, I was trying to keep the house clean. That was a joke. Planning the funeral felt like I was playing make believe. Like a bad dream. Even when it was time to rest, I could not rest because I was thinking too much. I asked myself was this real? I wanted this to be a dream. Family and friends were all over the place helping with everything. But at night the house was so quiet. I did not want to go to sleep, nor did I want to eat. My mind began racing, Why did you have to leave so soon? Were you trying to tell me something when we were talking the morning you went to be with God?

I remember making a few trays of food for the repast. Planning a funeral for your loved one requires a lot of time and attention. In addition, you've got to make decisions and be clear on what you want done or have to do during the planning process.

What was it like for you to plan a funeral for your loved one?

_____

_____

_____

_____

_____

_____

_____

_____

_____

_____

_____

_____

_____

_____

_____

_____

_____

_____

_____

_____

_____

_____

_____

Chapter 3

THE DAY OF THE FUNERAL

I REMEMBER LOTS of people. I remember he was wearing a chocolate-colored suit, looking handsome as ever. I remember my youngest child crying and my friend grabbed him. I remember hugging Curtis while beside the casket and he smelled like cold steel. I remember my co-workers leading the funeral procession. I remember everyone helping out. I remember the weather was very cold. I remember it felt like a show because it definitely did not seem like my husband was gone to be with Jesus. I remember people saying, "I am sorry for your loss" and I looked at them like *this is just a dream*. I remember my 4-year-old at the funeral saying, "Wake Daddy up! Daddy is sleep." That truly broke my heart.

After the funeral when everyone went home, I locked the house and attempted to go to bed. Not happening. I was up all night. I was hoping that I would hear him pull up to the house, hearing the music from the car radio when he pulled in front. Then he was walking through the front door. I was hoping that I would wake up from the nightmare

I was having. This felt so fake. Life was like a blur. The funeral is over, reality is still not setting in. The house is quiet. Sleep is interrupted by every little sound that I hear.

After a few weeks phone calls were not as frequent from family or friends. Where is my soulmate? When will I wake up from this dream I am having? I feel so sad all the time. Wake up! Wake up! From this terrible dream. Tears, tears, more tears. The children are so sad all the time. I am so used to helping others solve their problems but not this time. I needed help. I just felt so hopeless and helpless.

What do you remember about the funeral for your loved one? What did you do after the funeral?

_____
_____
_____
_____
_____
_____
_____
_____
_____
_____
_____
_____
_____
_____
_____
_____

I KNOW WHAT YOU ARE GOING THROUGH

Chapter 4

———✺———

Grief Phases

Daze

THROUGH EACH WEEK and month everyone will go through the phases of grief at a different pace or they may even skip a phase. For me I think I went through every phase over a five-year period. I did not realize that I was even going through these phases until years had passed. I was reading about grief and I was like *Oh yeah, I went through that...* I went through phases and then I would sometimes return back to the 2nd or 3rd phase. There's no rhyme or reason why; it just happens. The one thing about being in the grief family is that life continues to go on—we encounter people whether we like it or not. Trust me when I tell you that I know what you are going through. The best advice to get through these phases is to just GRIEVE! It's ok. You got to do it.

Upon finding out about the loss of your loved one—you are immediately in a complete daze. It feels like you are just not going to make it. You are in total disbelief...

Did you go through this phase? How did you feel?

_____

_____

_____

_____

_____

_____

_____

_____

_____

_____

_____

_____

_____

_____

_____

_____

_____

_____

_____

_____

_____

_____

DENIAL

Denial is not accepting what is happening. The death of your loved one seems so unreal. Here are a few words that can be substituted for denial: avoidance, confusion, shock, fear. You are like *Noooooooooo!* You are numb and not trying to hear nothing anyone has to say. You often avoid conversation. You feel like fighting. You feel like screaming. You feel a great need to do something. You just cannot accept that this has happened. Anything that anyone said was a lie. For years I went to the doctors asking questions about my heart, trying to seek answers in reference to why my husband had a heart attack. Probably after the fourth or fifth time, the doctor sat me down and explained to me that it was his time and that even if he had made it to the hospital, the heart attack may still have happened. I told him, "No, it would not." I was in straight denial. I did not want to hear or know the truth. Causes of death go on and on. Maybe there was a whole different cause for the death in your life. However, it's relatable because we lost our loved one.

Have you gone through denial? Do you feel like your loved one is coming back? Do you sometimes avoid conversations?

_____
_____
_____
_____
_____
_____
_____
_____
_____
_____
_____
_____
_____

_____

_____

_____

_____

_____

_____

_____

_____

_____

_____

_____

_____

_____

_____

_____

ANGER

After denial had run its course, I became very angry. I was frustrated and irritated. I just couldn't let it go. I remember going to bed angry and waking up furious. Why are we angry? We are angry because the death may have been sudden, expected, unexpected, tragic... Whatever the case, our loved one is not here and we are very ANGRY!!!! We are angry because it's someone we cherish.

I was angry because we were supposed to grow old together. I was angry because our loved one took care of us. He loved us.

I was angry at friends who I thought should have been there for me. I was angry that this was not a bad dream from which I could awaken.

I remember being at the mall with my kids and I would get angry at other families because it was mom, dad, and children, and for me it was just mom and children. I was even mad at God. I was doing something

I knew was wrong; I was questioning God—I was accusing him. I had to come to my senses and get it together because I knew that God don't make no mistakes.

Every time I thought about the whole death scenario, anxiety took over my mind and body. My heart felt like it would burst out of my chest.

What were you angry about? Are you still angry? What do you think would have made it better?

_____

_____

_____

_____

_____

_____

_____

_____

_____

_____

_____

_____

_____

_____

_____

_____

_____

_____

_____

_____

BARGAINING

I put the blame on myself for a very long time. I should have done this; I should have done that. Why did I go to the store? I should have taken him to the store with me. It's my fault. Why? Why? Why? Why? Why was all that was going through my mind. I remember saying God please wake me up from this bad dream, I will be more obedient to your word. I will work harder for you Lord. Please God bring my love one back. If you do this ....I will do this........... I did this for quite a while. I said DAMN quite often.

Have you done some bargaining? Did you blame yourself or someone else?

_____

_____

_____

_____

_____

_____

_____

_____

_____

_____

_____

_____

_____

_____

_____

_____

_____

_____

DEPRESSION

From the moment my loss occurred, I entered into a deep state of depression.

There is no set time frame when depression will strike. I know with me, as I look back, it came when no one was around and the funeral was long over. The greeting cards stopped, phone calls stopped,and people stopped coming by like they use to. As my mind had idle time, I began drifting into a deep depression—then a deeper one. I thought I would not recover from this. I remember one time my oldest child told me, "Mom, me and my siblings still have to eat."

I felt so bad because we had been eating fast foods, cereal, or something they could easily make. I had the bank card on the dresser so they could easily order food. Cooking was the last thing on my mind. I fought my way back enough just to begin cooking my kids a meal. I remember the last words from my husband. He said, "If anything happens to me, take care of my children and live out my legacy." I figured them eating was part of taking care of my kids, so I gave it a try. I began cooking for my kids. They were so happy. I really had to push myself out of bed to take care of my responsibilities.

Depression is expected after a loss. We get so used to living a certain way and within a blink of an eye our lives have been changed. It was like *what in the world just happened?* I went from this happy wife to being depressed, to angry, and then back to depressed. It was going to take time. God said, "Weeping may endure for a night but joy comes in the morning" (Psalm 30:5).

I felt like lying around all the time--not wanting to be around people. Not wanting to socialize. I just wanted to dream about Curtis. I wanted to dream that he was still here. Insomnia was my middle name. I felt hopeless. I was always in the WHY? Why this? Why that?

What is going on in your mind right this minute? What were some of the last words your loved one said to you?

_____

_____

_____

_____

_____

_____

_____

_____

_____

What makes you feel better?

_____

_____

_____

_____

_____

_____

_____

_____

_____

ACCEPTANCE

A question that comes to my mind today is: when do you accept that your loved one is not coming back? When do you say, "Ok I am at peace with this. Let's move on"? When do you let go of the guilt, the hurt and the pain. When? When? When? This, to me, was the hardest phase. There is not a day that goes by that you will not think about your loved one. Not one day. It doesn't matter if it's a year or much longer. In twenty years, a thought about your loved one will pop into your mind at the strangest moment...

As I look back, I would say that I tried to avoid the acceptance phase. I did not want to accept the fact that Curtis was gone. I did not want anyone to say that he has gone to a better place. When people would bring up a conversation about my love one, I would say, "He is not gone." He's on vacation. He will be back. Even during grief counseling, I would say sometimes in conversation, "When he left..." People would ask *where did he go?*

You do not have a time limit. When the acceptance finally happens you will know it. Losing my loved one did not sink in until long after.

Have you accepted the fact that your loved one is gone? What are some of the things that you have said to people that ask you, "How are you doing? What have you been up to?"

_____

_____

_____

_____

_____

_____

_____

_____

_____

_____

_____

_____

_____

_____

_____

_____

_____

_____

_____

_____

_____

_____

_____

_____

Chapter 5

GRIEF THERAPY

GRIEF WILL LEAVE you so exhausted. I was always crying, which led to the headaches, red eyes, digestion problems, trouble sleeping—which led to sleeping pills, overeating, or undereating. Multiple issues occurring all the time. Please seek the help. There are a lot of grief groups and also one-on-one sessions that will help you get through this most delicate and precious time in your life. Through this journey during our most precious time, it's ok to seek help. I will admit I went to counseling for three years. I did group and one-on-one; I enjoyed the group sessions the best. I even had the kids in grief counseling.

I know some people think they don't need it; however, it felt so good to know that I had someone to relate to. I have heard some people say they don't want to go through counseling because they don't want anyone to be in their business or they're tough enough or patient enough to wait it out. I definitely would recommend counseling. You will be surprised how helpful counseling can be. God put people in those positions to help us get through. Whether it's a group session or individual session, being with people is truly nourishing to the soul. Just think about it; we all are going through the same thing and just to know that someone else is going through something similar, thinking the same way we are, feeling the way we are... It's truly a blessing. I remember being in counseling talking with my group and I would be like, *Oh my goodness, I be thinking that way also or I be doing the same thing.* Please seek counseling. We are not alone on this journey called grief.

Have you been to grief counseling? What was your experience? If you have not been, what's stopping you?

Chapter 6

PEOPLE JUST DON'T KNOW!

PEOPLE JUST DON'T know what to say or do when trying to support you during your time of grief.

These are some of the things people may say during your grief journey:

When are you going to move on? or You need to move on.

Are you ok?

When are you going to get over this?

It's been six months.

It's been a year.

It's been two years.

You not finished going through this yet?

I know what you are going through.

I know how you feel.

I know what you mean.

At least you had someone to love you.

They are in a better place.

They right here.

Your loved one would not want you to be sad.

It was a blessing that you had him for the time you had him.

Your loved one would want you to get it together.

Get yourself together.

Do it for the kids.

She / or He fought the good fight.

You are so strong.

You got this.

It's ok.

I understand.

Look, now get it together.

He or she brought this on their self.

He lived a good life.

You should sell your house and move.

How can you stay in this house?

You need to pull yourself together.

I really thought you would be over this...

You didn't get rid of their stuff yet?

What's wrong now?

How can you stay isolated in this house?

You should buy another car.

And the list goes on and on...

I had to sit back for a moment and take a deep breath, because I was ready to have a mean conversation with some folks. I had to realize they just didn't know what to say. All they knew was that a good friend or family member of theirs was going through a tough time and they had no clue what to say to me. I realized later they were just trying to be there for me. Trust me when I say, I know what you are going through! It's ok to ask that person, "Can you just sit here with me in quiet, can you just listen, or help around the house?" People want to be there for us but have a hard time with not knowing what to say or how to say it.

What are some of the words or phrases that people say or have said that make you upset? How did it make you feel? What are some things that you would rather have heard people say?

_____

_____

_____

_____

_____

_____

_____

_____

_____

_____

_____

_____

_____

_____

_____

_____

_____

_____

_____

_____

_____

_____

_____

_____

_____

_____

Remember God sends Angels in all forms. It may be a letter, a card, a person, a hug, THE WORD!

John 5:4

"God is with you – wherever you may go and no matter what life brings."

Chapter 7

―――∞―――

PEOPLE ARE TOUGH

I CAN RECALL reminiscing about good times about eight months after my husband passed. A friend of mine told me: don't start it. Assuming that I was about to start crying. I was shocked. My friend told me, "Look, this is the first time I had to go through this." I was like…"This is my first time also." I can sit back and laugh about it now because we both were going through.

You are going to come across people who just don't know what to say or how to express it. You are going to come across people who are cruel and insensitive. You must hold on. People who are very close to you may become distant and people who were distant may become closer to you. Every situation is different.

The reason the person closer to you becomes distant is because they are afraid to say the wrong thing. Keep in mind that they still love you. They just don't know how to handle this situation. They don't like to see you hurting. Give them time, they will come around in their time. Until then, focus on the good times that you and your loved one had. Focus on the positive things that your loved one would want you to do.

I realized that someone who has never experienced a loss will want you to move on with your life quickly simply because they don't know what you're going through. It's like a separate world for mourners all by themselves. We think that everyone understands but they don't. We think everyone should stop doing what they're doing but they don't. We think THE WORLD WOULD STOP but it does not. It keeps going regardless. Trust me when I say, I know what you are going through!

Have you experienced this?

_____

_____

_____

_____

_____

_____

_____

_____

_____

_____

_____

_____

_____

_____

_____

_____

Chapter 8

━━━━━◆◆◆━━━━━

THE MIDNIGHT HOUR

THE MIDNIGHT HOUR is the hour when you have finished keeping yourself busy for the day, and you have nothing else to do but try and rest to prepare for the next day. The midnight hour is when we want and need to get our rest. The midnight hour is something that we don't want to face but we must face. Trust me it will come and when it comes you will know it. The midnight hour will come often, and during that time you may find yourself waking up from a dream or you may think you hear your loved one in the house. You may even call out your loved one's name. I used to feel like my Curtis was sitting on my bed. I know it sounds crazy but nothing will make sense right now because sometimes you won't know fact from fantasy. Other people may not understand what you're going through but trust me when I say I know what you are going through.

I can remember one time I thought I heard my loved one pull up in front of the house with his favorite music on and it was loud. I ran and peered out of the window but there was no one. Sometimes you may wake up every night at the same time--for example 3:00 a.m. every morning. It's like entering a different part of a story without the plot. It's like going through life just because you have to. But sometimes I was excited just to get into bed so I could feel my husband's presence. It was very comforting. The midnight hour may not be as comforting for everyone. Everyone will have different experiences.

One thing I can share is that facing the midnight hour years later, I realized that God wanted to spend time with me alone. He wanted me to talk to him, he wanted me all to himself. God and I. God allowed me to know that, "Yea, though I walk through the valley of the shadow of death, I will fear no evil; for thou art with me; thy rod and thy staff they comfort me" (Psalms 23:4).

Have you experienced any of this? How have your midnight hours been? Please share.

_____

_____

_____

_____

_____

_____

_____

_____

_____

_____

_____

_____

_____

I KNOW WHAT YOU ARE GOING THROUGH

Chapter 9

DREAMS

Dreams are going to come. It may take a few days, months, or years. Don't worry; they are going to come. And they are going to appear so real. You are going to try and go back to sleep to pick up where the dream left off. When you can't pick up where you left off, you are going to sense different emotions. You may even find yourself getting very angry. You are going to try and figure out the message that is attempting to be sent. You may find yourself waking up a family member or close friend to tell them about the dream.

When the dreams do come, write them down in your journal, note the date and time of the dream, how you felt after the dream, what the dream was about. I remember dreaming within the first month about my husband telling me in the dream that he was so sorry that he passed away but he had to go. He never spoke in the dream but his actions and his look showed how sorry he felt. He hugged me so tight in the dream, it felt real. I woke up happy, then so sad. I had lots of dreams and described everyone of them on paper. You will have a lot of dreams.

Record when they happen. I use to try to go to sleep fast, so that I could dream of him. Trust and believe when I say I know what you are going through. This thing called grief is real and no one will have the same walk as everyone else; it will be similar but not 100% the same.

Have you had any dreams lately? When? Where did the dream take place? What happened? How did you feel after the dream? Even after utilizing this space, start writing down all your dreams in your journal. Begin writing because it will help you as you heal.

_____

_____

_____

_____

_____

_____

_____

_____

_____

_____

_____

_____

_____

_____

_____

_____

_____

_____

_____

_____

_____

_____

_____

_____

_____

_____

_____

Chapter 10

———— ∽ ————

WEEPING

"Weeping may endure for a night but joy cometh in the morning" (Psalm 30:5).

THINKING BACK ON the date of death is going to seem like it was just yesterday. Usually when it's a month or two weeks away, some may relive each significant moment up until the date of passing. It won't be easy. There will be happy moments and there may be tears.

I can remember every night about 3:00 a.m. my alarm to the house would go off. I'd gather all four of my kids and put them in one room and search my house every night. But I knew it was him. After I finished searching the house I'd get back into the bed with my lights on and then my husband would sit at the foot of my bed again the same as in the midnight hour. This went on for a long time. I would just move my legs over and feel him sit next to me. Call me crazy, but that's what I used to do.

I can remember my then 5-year-old son, Curreem, telling me to call

Jesus so that he could talk to his dad and my then 2 ½-year-old son, Curron, yelling up the steps, calling for Daddy. Those moments will never be forgotten.

I can remember going to the kids' events at school or football games, feeling sad because he wasn't there to share those moments. I would get upset seeing other mothers and fathers together while I was by myself. 1 John 5:4 states, "God is with you – wherever you may go and no matter what life brings."

I would ask God, "Why do the good people leave so soon?"

But I thank God for Jesus. I could not or would not have made it if it wasn't for the Lord My Savior, Jesus Christ. God said, "I will never leave you nor forsake you. I am a God that sits high and looks low. No weapon formed against you shall prosper."

What are your plans for your first year anniversary or what did you do during the first year anniversary after your loved one left you?

_____

_____

_____

_____

_____

_____

_____

_____

_____

_____

_____

_____

Chapter 11

———— ✺ ————

CREATING MEMORIES

UNLESS YOU DON'T celebrate holidays, they are coming whether you're ready or not. Even still, you will have important dates and milestones that you can't help but think of, reminisce about, and even celebrate.

I can remember after Curtis' death all of the significant holidays rolled around within that first year. First it was each of the kids' birthdays. Then it was our 14th wedding anniversary in May. Father's Day, and his birthday again in October. Then came Thanksgiving, Christmas, New Years and guess what? Here comes his date of death again—January 18. Year after year, no matter what, those dates were coming.

I say all of this because these special moments and holidays will come and go every year, possibly leaving you feeling hopeless and empty inside. I am here as a living testimony to tell you that the precious moments you had with your special someone will always be a part of you. There won't be a day that goes by that you won't think about your loved one. Take a few minutes right now or however long it might take you to reminisce about those special moments together.

When you feel up to it, write out a moment or moments that you will never forget:

_____

_____

_____

_____

_____

_____

_____

_____

_____

_____

_____

_____

_____

_____

_____

_____

_____

_____

_____

_____

_____

_____

_____

_____

_____

_____

_____

I want to share a few memory-creating exercises that you can enjoy:

MEMORIAL DAY CELEBRATION

God is truly amazing in my life. I thank God for us. I know that He is going to bring you through this most precious moment in your life. I pray that everyone who is reading this book will be blessed abundantly and stay covered in the name of Jesus. I pray that God comforts you and that you allow God to guide you according to his will. Remember God knows everything. IN JESUS' PRECIOUS NAME I PRAY, AMEN.

HEBREWS 11:1 STATES "NOW FAITH IS THE SUBSTANCE OF THINGS HOPED FOR, THE EVIDENCE OF THINGS NOT SEEN."

One Memorial Day, I helped create a memorial garden in the front of my house. I started near the end of March and it was finished by the end of May. It was beautiful. I invited everyone over to the house for a Memorial Day cookout. I had assistance making a big heart in the middle of the garden using white stones. Once everyone arrived, the kids had t-shirts on with their Dad's picture on it. I'd given each attendee a balloon. When everyone was ready, toward the end of the celebration, I announced, "EVERYONE WHO HAS LOST SOMEONE, ON THE COUNT OF THREE WE ARE GOING TO RELEASE THE BALLOONS AND SCREAM OUT THE PERSON'S NAME WHO WE LOST."

It was incredible. Dozens of different names were being yelled out, the balloons floated up into the beautiful sky. People were smiling and crying all at the same time. That moment will never be forgotten.

Take lots of photos. **Create a Scrapbook. Get multiple copies of the photos so that you can share with anyone else who wants pictures.**

This is a good project for the kids also. Everyone can have their scrapbook for years to come and then pass them on to their children. **Create a collage/ Make a poster**

Organize a 5K race in your loved one's memory or find a 5k race or walk and participate in their memory

Create a College fund

Think of something that your loved one enjoyed and create one, using whatever materials you can come up with, or donate to a charity something they had a passion for.

Living out your special person's Legacy

Did your loved one have a special project, business, or anything that they were working on or enjoyed doing? Live out their legacy, research or reach out to family and friends and see if they can help you with it. Doing something in your loved one's memory will not only make you feel happy but it will definitely help you reach different levels of comfort and coping with your loss. In addition, it creates a memory that will last forever.

Celebrate your loved one's birthday, anniversary, Father's day or Mother's Day

Sometimes you may just want to hang out in the house or go outdoors for a little while.

I know during my first few years I would have a "loved one's" day. That day would consist of putting on my loved one favorite shirt, jewelry, or a spray of his cologne. I would fix or order his favorite meal and/or drink, listen to favorite songs or watch his favorite movie. I would just relax and think about the good times. I would write in my journal. And if it was his birthday, I would sing and eat birthday cake. Sometimes I invited close relatives and sometimes I celebrated with just me and the kids.

You can do this; let's create memories

Share your thoughts: what are some things you have done or would like to do:

_____

_____

_____

_____

_____

_____

_____

_____

_____

_____

_____

_____

_____

_____

_____

_____

_____

_____

_____

_____

_____

_____

_____

_____

_____

_____

_____

_____

Chapter 12

WHAT DO WE DO NOW?

Deuteronomy 31:6

"Be strong and of a good courage, fear not, nor be afraid of them; for the Lord thy God, he that doth go with thee; he will not fail thee, nor forsake thee."

OUR LIVES HAVE just been changed forever. What do we do now? How can we go on with our lives when a part of us just passed away? I can remember going outside to run errands one Saturday morning and I realized anew that my loved one was not here anymore with me. He really was gone. Who was going to go to the store with me? Who was going to help with the kids? Who? When my loved one was here with me, life was happy, it was like, "Let's do this together and do that together. Where are we going tonight?" Now since my loved has gone to be with the Lord, I have to go do what I have to do while feeling empty inside. I do errands and then go straight back home. How can people go on with their lives? I am hurting, why are people still smiling, laughing and eating. Don't they know I am hurting. I feel like screaming.

Then I wait, maybe he will walk through the door. Maybe he will call and say, "I am right here." The world did not stop moving because I lost my loved one. Anxiety ripped through me on a regular basis. I thought I would not make it. But God has been carrying me through this grief walk.

The grief walk is a community all by itself. I began researching and I found some grief peer support groups in the area in which I lived. I went through three different grief sessions for three years. I must say it definitely paid off. I met a lot of people that were going through the same grief that I was going through. In one particular group we would talk about different things we were going through and what we were facing. While the conversation was going on I would say, "Oh my goodness, I was thinking the same thing." I even found grief support for my kids. The support for kids would meet weekly and have group discussions and they were also given the ability to talk about their loved one. The kids really benefited from the group meets.

My dear cousin began to send me scriptures about mourning and the comfort that comes through our Lord and Savior, Jesus Christ. I began reading scriptures day in and day out. I began talking to the Lord more and more. The weight of sadness began to lift off me. It was a lengthy process. But all I can say is that God is AWESOME! When we put our trust in God, he will carry us through the storm, the heartache and the pain. God said he will never leave us nor forsake us.

Chapter 13

———— ❧ ————

VULNERABLE MOMENTS

ACCORDING TO DICTIONARY.COM, being vulnerable means being susceptible to physical or emotional attack or harm. Basically, it is being weak and without protection. Being susceptible to do things you don't want to do. Falling for anything you think is the right thing to do, but in reality, it may be wrong timing or the wrong thing to do. Whatever you do, please rethink major decisions. Please don't jump, run, and do things without God in the mix of your plans. It's so sad but true; people will do it every time. Some may try to defraud you. They might use you. They may look for an opportunity to take advantage of a vulnerable person. Sometimes it's a person you have known for a long time or perhaps a short while. It can be a family member, including your kids. But just in case it is, please pray before making major decisions. A lot of times the thoughts in your mind go crazy. Of course, the mind is the creator of all the thoughts that you have. I can remember certain individuals used me for money. They never paid me back. Someone may push you to get into a relationship when you are not ready, because you are so vulnerable. A lot of times people prey on the weak. So please, please be careful.

There are people we call "controllers" who may try to coerce you to adjust your whole lifestyle to their's. People may attempt to convince you to do things you are not ready to do. Psalm 46:10 says, "Be still and know that I am God." During these vulnerable moments, we really need to be still and wait on the Lord. When big decisions need to be made, we need to wait and listen for God's voice. The Lord said, "We have not because we ask not." When we try to handle things on our own, THEY DON'T WORK! BUT WHEN WE ASK THE LORD, HE WILL SHOW UP AND TAKE CARE OF US. HE IS AN ON TIME GOD!

Please keep in mind that its not everybody. There are a lot of genuine and righteous people in the world.

"Do not be anxious about anything, but in everything by prayer and supplication with thanksgiving let your requests be made known to God" (Philippians 4:6).

Have you experienced any of these moments? Let's talk about it.

_____

_____

_____

_____

_____

_____

_____

_____

_____

_____

_____

_____

Chapter 14

ONE MORE

SINCE THE LOST of my loved one I have been living my life moment by moment. I learned that planning all the time does not work. Of course, we can't go and spend all the rent money. However, what I did learn was that God is a Guaranteed God, and he promises to never ever leave us. My new outlook on life is to enjoy life with my loved ones every day and say, 'I love you' daily. Hold onto the memories because that's what's going to keep us moving forward. Moments are very special. Please hold on to them.

If you had one more day or one more moment with your loved one, what would that day or moment be like? What would you say? What would you do differently?

_____

_____

_____

_____

_____

_____

_____

_____

_____

_____

_____

_____

_____

_____

_____

_____

_____

_____

_____

_____

_____

_____

_____

If your response made you feel a great deal of guilt or if it put you in a stage of 'I should of, could of, or would of' moment, please, let that guilt go. It's going to make you sick, stressed and depressed. What helped me was the realization that God knows everything. God says there is a time to be born, a time to die, a time for everything under the sun. There is a time to cry and a time to laugh. There is a time to be sad and a time to dance. There is a time to look for something and a time to stop looking for something. There is a time to keep things and a time to throw things away. (Ecclesiastes 3; some scriptures from verses 1-10). God knows. God knows we are going to hurt, but he says I am your comforter. He sends people to help comfort you. You will find comfort in Gods word. Your mind is going to be all over the place, but we must take control and think positive thoughts. If we allow our mind to wander onto the negative that's going to make it more difficult to get through. I thought I would not get through this terrible moment in my life, BUT GOD! I can say that after journaling for 3 ½ years, after 3 years of grief counseling (regular and group), after just giving my entire life and self to God—my load got lighter. I am thankful to be able to write and assure you that God will and can get you through EVERYTHING. After you have journaled for about one to three years, go back and read your journal. You are going to be surprised just how far you've come. You are going to look back and say GOD is soooooo good. Just know that there is not one day that I don't think about my loved one--NOT ONE! However, I try to think about all the good times.

Have you given your entire life to Christ? Do you trust God that he will see you through? Please answer honestly, this is between you and God. God has your back.

_____

_____

_____

_____

_____

_____

_____

_____

_____

_____

_____

_____

_____

_____

Chapter 15

YOU ARE WORTHY!

WE MUST BELIEVE all of God's promises

Romans 8:28

"And we know that in all things God works for the good of those who love him, who have been called according to his purpose."

Hebrews 13:3

"I will never leave you or forsake you."

Jeremiah 29:11

"I know the plans I have for you declares the Lord, Plans to prosper you and not to harm you, plans to give you hope and a future."

Jeremiah 31:3

"I have loved you with an everlasting love."

Hebrews 13:8

"Jesus Christ is the same yesterday and today and forever."

John 17:17

"Sanctify them by the truth; your word is truth."

John 14:27

"Peace I leave with you, my peace I give you. I do not give to you as the world gives. Do not let your hearts be troubled and do not be afraid."

Isaiah 40:29

"He gives strength to the weary and increases the power of the weak."

Isaiah 40:31

"But those who hope in the Lord will renew their strength."

John 3:16

"For God so loved the world that he gave his one and only Son, that whoever believes in him shall not perish but have eternal life."

Please know that you are worthy! Despite everything that you are going through, you are worthy! God's promises are forever. Think about your loved one as well and ask yourself this question: What would my loved one want me to do? How would they want me to try my best to take care of ME! Please share. You can do this!

_____

_____

_____

_____

_____

_____

_____

_____

_____

_____

_____

_____

_____

_____

_____

_____

_____

_____

_____

_____

_____

_____

_____

I want to encourage you to please don't not give up. I thought that was the way to go until God told and showed me otherwise. When you allow God to work in your life in either good or bad times, he will comfort and carry you through the storm in Jesus' name. God Bless you!

CPSIA information can be obtained
at www.ICGtesting.com
Printed in the USA
BVHW040940060620
581011BV00015B/983